SEASONS
OF THE SOUL

A MESMERIZING AND POETIC BATTLE WITH
POST TRAUMATIC STRESS DISORDER

SHERI J. MICHEL

VMH

VMH Vikki M. Hankins™ Publishing
www.vmhpublishing.com

Book Cover Design by Vikki Jones
Book Cover Image: Shutterstock
Interior Design by VMH Publishing

VMH Vikki M. Hankins™ Publishing is a registered trademark, and the publisher of this work. For information about special discounts for bulk purchases, please contact VMH Publishing specials sales at info@vmhpublishing.com.

Publisher's Note:

The publisher is not responsible for the content of this book nor websites, or social media pages (or their content) that are not owned by the publisher.

Manufactured in the United States of America

10 9 8 7 6 5 4 3 2 1

Hardback ISBN: 978-1-947928-88-6
Paperback ISBN: 978-1-947928-89-3

Contents

Prologue

Spring, summer, fall, and winter; these are the seasons of time. The breathtaking view of new flowers, the warmth of the sun, the smell of bonfires, and the freshness of the first snowfall all have some sort of significant meaning to all of us. There are also seasons of the soul. These are the seasons where we begin, where we stand still, and where we chose whether we take a path or set out on a journey. Paths lead us in all directions, some straight and sure, some narrow and winding, some rocky and treacherous. Journeys bring us the experiences of life and mold us into who or what we become.

This is the stage of my life where I have realized there is nothing more than a moment. For therein lies truth. I have this one chance to be, one chance to be free, to be me. I have stepped out from behind the wall. In this final stage of my life, I will take and accept what every part of me senses is right for me. Is that selfish?

If I take one final chance on all that is

and all that I feel, will I lose? There are some serene moments of solitude that fear does still cloud my vision, and I am unsure. But what is there to lose but fear, the fear of stepping out, of stepping beyond what is safe and into what is unknown. What is there to lose but fear? Fear keeps us all at bay. The fear of the things we can't expect and sometimes of things we can't accept. I accept that there is nothing more for me than that which I feel, for I finally feel with every part of me all that is within the five senses of self and all that is within the one sense of my soul. I have longed to be free to be who I am and not ever be afraid to allow myself to do so. To feel sure that there is really one person who will totally and realistically accept me for who I am. That person is me.

There are parts of me that make up a dark side, a light side, and a gray side. We all have parts of us that are frightening, yet most of us are so afraid to be. For what would people think, what would they say? Sometimes I care, sometimes I don't, and sometimes I bask in the emptiness that I have created for myself out of that fear. No more.

When you close your eyes what do you dream? Do you dream of riches and materialistic items that you can replace over and over again? Do you dream of finding a place where you are safe to feel and safe to be what could possibly be simply a destiny? Never laugh at anyone's dreams, for those who don't dream don't have much. In the brightness of day, when I dream, I see a place; it is some place where I can be soft and warm, cold and heartless, yet peaceful and a little bit evil all at the same time. Even at a given moment, I can change. As long as I am real, I would be accepted for what I feel and for who I am. No masks, no pretending, no softening the blow; only reality and only what is me. I see a place with honesty, integrity, and compassion; and yet truth to self is the only reality.

This is a journey of souls; a journey with trails of sorrow, need, longing, light, and darkness. Travel through the seasons and remember that the eyes are truly a mirror of the soul, and truth does lie in a moment.

Chapter 1

The Four Seasons

I sat in the silence, gazing at one mirror that was split in two separate sides. My hands were folded neatly and pristinely in my lap. This is the way I was taught because appearances are everything. I held my body straight and erect, leaning forward slightly in an attempt to calm the shaking. On one side of the mirror was a reflection that I recognized. One eye still sparkled with strength. I looked closer to see if the eye still glittered with laughter when I tried to smile. There was something missing, but I couldn't quite find what it was because my mind was still reeling. The only sound I heard was the slight ticking of the digital clock. Then as if to ease the silence, I laughed out loud. Since when did digital clocks make a sound?

I turned my head slightly to see the other side, the separate side. The eye was dull and lifeless, skin blackened and swollen underneath. I raised a now shaking hand and willed it to touch the face the mirror reflected.

My fingers instead touched the glass and felt wetness as if the tears in my eyes were only reality in the image. "Shake it off," I said to my reflection. "You can do this. Just breathe."

Two deep breaths and exhale slowly I thought. With a now steady hand, I tried to prepare myself for the day. Calmly I wiped the tears away and then in a fit of despair, threw the makeup down. What did it matter anyway? Even if I didn't cover the bruises, no one would notice, no one would ask. It wouldn't be proper now would it to ask if I was okay.

Just as I turned away in an attempt to leave the reality of my reflection in the mirror, there was a soft yet persistent knock on the bedroom door. Knowing who was on the other side, I took one gaze back; and what I saw in my reflection this time sent shivers up my own spine. The room was no longer mirrored beyond my image. There was simply empty space, full of an icy fog that seemed to pulsate in the darkness. It was like the sting of an icy winter chill swept into the room, and I knew that I had been here before. I had been in this place, in the mirrored image, which now reflected eyes that were empty and as cold as the frost that suddenly appeared on the glass.

The knock was heard again, and then reality as I wrapped myself tighter in the thick robe willing it to provide the warmth I so desperately needed. I shook my head to bring myself back into the present, wincing uncontrollably in pain as the throbbing under my blackened eye brought the salty sting of tears. With all the strength I thought I could ever have, I willed my feet to steady and whispered just soft enough to ease the pounding, "Never again will I be herein this place. Never again."

"Let me in. We need to talk." The sound of his voice chilled me even more. Like a trapped animal sensing danger, I could smell the fear. Its stale sourness choked me. My body rocked back in shocked disbelief as I recognized the bitter taste of fear in the air. "Open the door. Now!" he said.

I released the lock, opened the door and walked backwards into the darkened room. Gathering what strength I could muster from the slim thread of satisfaction I got suddenly knowing he was the one who brought the taste and smell of fear into the room, I almost smiled. I almost laughed out loud, but it wasn't time. There was too much to do. I turned around to face him, head high, chin defiant, and in a voice even I didn't recognize I said, "No one, not even you, will ever do this to me again."

He came towards me, arms outstretched. The tears in his eyes made me nauseated. "You made me do it. I'm sorry, it will never happen again. I'm not leaving this house. It's mine, and I pay for it." Then he had the audacity to say, "I love you. I can't be without you. It will never happen again."

How many times had I heard that, forgotten, and gone on pretending? I had lost track of the holes in the wall, the angry words, the blame, the condescending words, and the threats. "I don't care what you do," I said, "I'm going to work." He put his hand out to stop me but caught himself and said, "What are you going to say? You can't go out looking like that. What are you going to say?" I must have been crazy, just like he would tell me, because this time I actually laughed at him and said, "Nothin'. They never do, so it really doesn't matter, does it?"

I ran down to the garage before he could stop me, before the typical fear of what he would do changed my mind. I thought back to the night before when I told him to leave afterwards, when I called my family in hysterics saying he hit me. The last thing I remembered before falling into some black hole of nothingness was their reply, "He would never do that. What did you do?"

I knew I shouldn't go to work, but I couldn't help it. I had to drive. I loved driving that car. The one he said I shouldn't have because it wasn't "proper." I loved the tight gearshift, the power of the V8 engine, the still new smell of black leather, and the freedom of the wind through my hair when the top was down. It was barely 55 degrees outside, but I hit the power button for the drop top anyway and was out of the driveway with it only part way down.

I revved the engine, shifted through the low gears, and spun around the corner headed for the freeway. The outer belt had more curves, so I took the long way around. Music blaring, heater blasting, I allowed my mind to free itself of all the confusion. I let all the ugliness rush off into the wind. After a while I exited the freeway, hit the gas, and traveled the narrow winding roads throughout the county. I was simply dodging the stars and chasing the moon. For now, I was free.

Two hours later, head high, I walked into the club. I smiled at the manager, waved at some clients, and said my usual "what's up" to my workout partners. I could feel my swollen eye throbbing; even I could see the blue blackness out of its corner. Just as I had expected, no one said a word. It hurt to smile, and it hurt that no one noticed; but I had pretended for so long now, and since even my own family blamed me, why would anyone else care. Why would a stranger, much less an acquaintance, ask if I was okay or much less care.

So I walked into the classroom, hit the fan switch, and checked all the bikes. I pulled out the cassette tape labeled "anaerobic" and gave the volume another turn. This class will be almost as good as the car ride, I thought, with just a bunch of regulars who do their own thing. All they wanted was to ride and feel, which was just what I needed.

Bob came in first; he always did. "What's up?" he said. "I had a frantic day at work, so crank up the volume for me will you?" "No problem," I said, without turning around, wincing a little as I smiled. Good ole Bob. The louder the music, the more he loved the class. Yeah, this will be just what the doctor ordered, I thought.

Seven more regulars swaggered in. Some were talking, some laughing, and some rushing to get set up, ready to start the ride. It was the late evening class, the one that only the die hards came to. Some were searching for release, some searching for that last bit of energy high, and some just looking for the comradery of a stealth workout after a long ass workday. As I gazed around the class, making sure everyone was set and rolling, I took a deep breath. As soon as I said the words I always did, they would all look up; and then I would know just how bad I really looked.

I turned down the music, said a quick and silent, "find your chi," looked up, and yelled, "Are you ready to ride?" All eight pairs of eyes looked up and, just as quickly, all eight pair looked down except for one. Bob: he has the only pair of eyes that held mine with something close to any feeling, be it anger or concern, just something other than the anticipation of the ride. Even he simply shook his head, and I knew he would never say another word. It was nice knowing, though, that maybe someone did give a shit.

Just as one tear broke free from the corner of my wounded eye, I turned the volume higher and said, "Bob had a bad day, and we're crankin' it up tonight." That night, in that class, they yelled louder, rode harder, and pedaled faster. Their faces were slick with sweat, and their leg muscles were taunt. I knew they were riding with me, riding to be free. "Give it more road, higher up the hill, strong legs," I spoke softly, just enough to be heard over the steady rhythm of the music as it drove them harder.

This was peace, this was feeling, this moment was everything I needed and more. The ride was on, and the class was into it. Somehow, through the sweat, the music, and the sweet pain of burning muscles, it all made sense. Nothing else mattered but the feeling of those 45 minutes when everyone busted ass to burn off the day. This was the one place where it didn't matter, and the only place where reality was in the moment.

Afterwards, after the cool down, the energetic smiles and the "thanks great class" after it was all said and done, I walked out with a lighter soul but a still heavy heart. I was back to real life, where condescending words and the game of cat and mouse was way too old. There were decisions to be made.

Had I known then what I know now, I would've ridden a little harder, driven a little longer, and walked away a little faster. Negatives come in threes.

And the seasons flash one by one in the shadows of my eyes.

Chapter 2

Winter

"You're so closed off. You won't even let me touch you. How are we supposed to work things out if I can't touch you?" If he said anything else, that was all I heard. He bought me presents, small tokens, flowers, and jewelry. I'd catch glimpses of days past in my dreams. Days when he moved suddenly, and I didn't flinch. I started working more, spending more hours working out just to be somewhere else but home with him. I couldn't stand to see him, hear his voice, or even smell him. I stopped going to family outings, stopped going out with friends, and started wearing sweats to bed because I was always so damn cold. The thought of him or anyone else touching me made me physically ill, and it seemed I always smelled that sourness of fear as if it were burned in my nostrils.

He told me he loved me. He promised he would never hit me again. Still, I kept silent. I shut myself off from everything as the months rolled on. I stopped pretending and somewhere along the line, I stopped caring. I only wanted out: I only wanted the freedom of the fast car ride, and the furious bike rides, and I only wanted to keep going somewhere, anywhere, and just never stop. But he controlled everything, and I kept wondering why I never noticed that before.

And still, I learned to stand still and straighter. I learned to stay silent and strong. I learned to brush off the pain of emptiness and the loss of what I believed was love. The days rolled on, and the nights of bitterness and angry words lengthened into weeks and months. Whenever the sun showed a hint of warmth, I was outside trimming trees, mowing, and weeding. I craved the sunshine; I longed for its warmth to soothe my soul. Since he controlled everything else, I taught myself to control the one thing I could – feeling. I became numb.

One early morning when he was out of town, I walked barefoot across the wooden deck trying to catch some of the sun's warmth and breathe it deep within me. I felt something sharp in the center of my foot, sat down, and turned my foot upwards to see a three inch piece of deck wood sticking out of the sole of my foot. I pulled it out watching my blood heavily travel down onto the deck, into the ground beneath where it soaked into the dirt. I knew I should wrap it, apply pressure, and make it stop. My blood was red, then dark, and I knew it should hurt. Yet, I was mesmerized by the flow. I wondered why I could bleed so much and never feel anything at all. So I wrapped my foot in a towel because I didn't want to make a mess. That's when I realized this is what my life was now; I had learned to will all pain away. I really was numb.

As the days and weeks crept by, I somehow lived in limbo, still always cold, still numb. I was surprised when I awoke one day feeling a stabbing pain in my lower abdomen. I told myself to will that pain away. But, it came back later, much more fierce; and I thought I could control it and will it away again. It kept coming, forcing its way around to my back and into my legs. Days and days, with each one I told myself, "this will pass."

One day when I doubled over from the pain, some door opened in the back of my mind, and I knew something wasn't right. I felt it deep within the crevice of my very soul, and I knew I didn't want to know. Living in a silent hell had taught me to trust my instinct, and this time my instinct said something was definitely wrong. I didn't know if I had the strength to face another setback, another hurdle. I had to take in the darkness or another wall that I had to climb alone. I almost hated that I felt that way, that I had to handle everything alone, everything silently alone.

The raging winter storm blasts its coldness through my eyes.

Chapter 3

Winter to Summer

"You have cancer," the doctor said. Negatives come in threes. There are battles you fight. There are some you win, some you lose, and some you would just as soon not be a part of. This was one I wanted no part of. Reaching down inside, I knew, or at least I thought I did, I could win this one. Yet part of me was reluctant to fight, and the other part of me...well, it was like I really didn't care. I thought I was a brave warrior, a solid soldier, a strong adversary. I could overcome this and even all that had come before. But then there was my defensive mode, one that blocked me from feeling the strength, blocked me from feeling anything at all except the need to run. Why is life sometimes so hard?

So I just focused. I shut myself off from everything that didn't have to do with the cancer. It wasn't that I just focused on beating it, I just had to focus on "it" because nothing else made sense either. My whole life wasn't mine anymore, the abuse, the betrayal, the pain, the cancer; it was someone else's.

I rebuilt some walls and built some taller and stronger ones. It seemed as if everyone else was telling me what to do, where and how to do it. I didn't want another surgery, and I didn't want radiation; I wanted to focus and simply believe in myself. I just wanted to be left alone and believe in the strength of my own power to control what was happening within me.

But I did have the surgery. The doctor told me it would make them know for sure that the cancer was gone. My husband, the one that had betrayed me over and over again, said "we" had to be sure. He said I was crazy if I didn't have the surgery. I knew the cancer was gone. I just did and I didn't want to….but I did because that was what was "expected." When would I learn to listen to me?

There were two surgeries within a month of each other. I'm sure others had been through worse, so who was I to complain. I can still smell the antiseptic aroma of the hospital room and hear the subdued sound of monitors, doors opening in the stillness, and the soft murmur of the night shift's conversation. I can still feel the need to be home and wondering where home was. I can still feel the need to be surrounded by things that were familiar to me, things I thought were so important and have since learned aren't justly so. There was just the cold that reminded me of winter. The coldness, the beginning of the end of long light, green trees, and the freshness of the cool fall air. For me, winter seemed to keep on taking over, still giving the cold that chills your bones and brings shivers that never seem to stop. The winter of the soul is that which never seems to bring warmth no matter how many blankets or how much fire you burn.

For two weeks I was trapped in the fog of nightmares that left me panting for breath and grasping for the hospital bed rails in attempts to pull myself out of the mist of hellish faces; their laughter ringing in my ears and their elongated frozen fingers burning my skin as they pulled me down into the darkened depths of fear. All those nightmares mixed in confusion with the drug induced dreamless sleep of peace; miles of open road, the wind at my back, me in the drop top, me on the bike, riding, driving with the suns warmth claiming me, healing me; me rolling away into the clouds.

I went home with the assurances of the doctor that the cancer was gone. I would have to have checkups every three months, but I was a success case. I was lucky. Why could I not shake the feeling that something was wrong, something was very wrong? Negatives come in threes.

The walls came tumbling down. There wasn't anything left but rubble. I was in the middle of the rubble, in the middle of dark ruins, which were both past and present. I had failed myself; I failed in what I truly believed. There was no one to blame but me.

You can live your life with courage, strength, and fortitude. You can live your life with hopes and dreams, and you can face your fears with truth, with your head high, and your eyes wide open. You can live the seasons of the soul with wonder, compassion for self, and anticipation of the next season; or you can continue within one particular season. Time can stand still while the days roll on, and for me, winter simply stood still.

Springs hope shines colorfully in my eyes.

Chapter 4

Winter

I couldn't feel the inside of my left leg. The pain in my lower abdomen was so intense at times I thought for sure I was dying. It felt like stabbing, pulsating needles of steel were buried just below the surface of the outside of my leg. My leg shook at times, and I would try to massage it or overcome the numbness and stop the shaking. I tried heat and ice. I pushed myself harder and harder. I just wanted to feel something other than pain. All the while I was wondering why the doctor said sometimes it happens. Sometime nerves get cut or severed. Did he have any idea what that meant? I couldn't even feel when I had sex. I couldn't feel anything, and I felt like I was filled with a black, charred lump of nothing. I felt dirty and contaminated, and I couldn't shake that damn feeling that something wasn't right.

So he was pissed again I wouldn't have sex, I spent too much time at the gym, and I spent too much time volunteering. I wanted to scream that I had just beaten cancer. I wanted to scream that this was his damn fault for "making" me have the second surgery. I wanted to blame someone, anyone…..instead I was silent.

Cry on the inside, laugh on the outside. My father told me that once, and I will never forget it. All throughout that long winter, I cried on the inside. I don't think I ever stopped.

I thought I had won a war. I believed I had won battles of abuse, of loss, of cancer, of solitude, and of guilt. I thought I was still standing. I chased the unknown and battled demons only I saw. I was ridiculed and abandoned. I was selfish and insane. I thought I left the coldness; I thought I left the bruised part of me behind. Little did I know that winter was still with me because its fierce storm was still sweeping through my soul. I wasn't standing at all; I was leaning between tattered shards of strength held together by the frozen pieces that were scattered within me.

I couldn't stand to have anyone touch me. I couldn't stand to have anyone near. I didn't realize what he had caused, what the cancer had left even though it was gone. I didn't think that I had lost control until I broke down. All the anger, all the tears still wouldn't melt the ice that had frozen inside me. I was leery of every one, of everything. As much as I wanted to be held, to be comforted, the thought of someone near me sent my body shaking with an intense....fear? I tried, I tried to trust, I tried to feel warmth, but I just couldn't. For some insane reason, I couldn't. I would cringe when someone got too close; I would step back and increase the distance cherishing my vast personal space. Just one time I tried to reach out; I wanted so desperately to feel. I wanted to feel the summer, even the spring, anything but the winter. Anything but the cold; I still felt so cold inside.

The pain never stopped. It consumed and the darkness settled again. With every step, with a sudden movement, even lying still at night, the pain was there. I went to so many doctors and therapists, and I tried new treatments and different tests, and no one could determine the cause. I was beginning to think it was all in my head. Maybe I was crazy, and maybe I was losing my mind. I hated myself, and I hated what I was, weak and dull. Weak, I hated weakness. I felt lifeless, yet some days when I summoned some of that buried strength,I went places. I searched for the part of my soul I had lost.

Years later, after many winters had passed, I found answers. Although the answer wasn't what I was hoping, it still provided closure. Maybe winter would finally move on. I would never feel part of my leg, and I would always hurt because there was too much damage to the nerves. There were adhesions and scar tissue that would probably come back continuously, spreading throughout my pelvic area. There were stiffening muscles, tightening tendons until the pain would sometimes spread, and then maybe shift making me believe it would go away. The times when my leg gave out or the pain doubled me over, I would laugh. What else could I do? It would come so suddenly, and I was so tired of crying. The tears were all dried up, and if I laughed, maybe they wouldn't come back. I was tired of being weak, and I was so very tired of being alone. I didn't deserve this, and I was tired of fighting. It was time to move on, and it was time to let the season change.

Yet still, winter stayed. The darkness overcame and the coldness settled deep inside. I tried to feel warmth; there was always hope and, in the end, despair. The end has finally come, and the steel coldness captivated my soul. Winter was here, and it was never going away. Always constant was the pain while my soul was spiraling downward into the darkness closed and alone.

Is it time to move on when the fire does fail to warm you? Is it time to move on when the stars have lost their luster and the beauty of the mountains loses its strength to calm? I have chosen to fight my secret battles by myself. Sure, I had the thought that I could survive it all alone. Instinct has served me well and taught me that battles can be won, but the war goes on. Today, in this long winter, the season that never seems to end, I have lost the strength to fight alone. Yet that is still where I am, where I know

I am destined to be. Dramatic and frightening is the reality of winter. There are times during this season that I am certain I am losing my mind. I sit in solitude and stare off into the starless sky, trying to remember summer, spring, and even fall. Times when there was warmth and trust, seasons of love, and seasons of faith. I longed for the winter to end and for spring to begin. I ached to feel and to see the goodness of beginnings, the clean smell of light rain showers that bring the sparkle of dew on a freshly cut lawn. I craved the season where souls are renewed and alive with laughter and joy. I only wanted to be. I only wanted to be something other than cold and alone and now frightened and scared. I wanted this because I knew that within the steel coldness of what I had become, I had lost myself; I had lost my will to be. After all I have done, after all that I have lost and given up and left behind, did I really deserve more than this season? I doubt it.

I do believe that winter has set in my soul. I do believe that I am no more. No illusions, no dreams, no hope, the only thing I feel is cold. I don't wish for death; I wish to no longer be. I wish to no longer be where there are hopeless fantasies that will never become reality. I wish to be where I can't be hurt, where I can't be misled, where I no longer have to fight to be. I wish for the heat of summer, a place where my soul can be warm and I can be free, yet still be alone. For that is my destiny, to be alone.

The need to run is overwhelming. I need to run where the pain isn't and where the heartache is no more. I need to go where there is no tomorrow, and there is no promise of tomorrow, and there is no promise of spring. I will never have a final spring, a breathtaking fall for there is only the heat of pain and the coldness of being truly alone. I am done, and the time is now to accept what fate has brought me. Battles that go on and wars that never end… battles of dark forbidden demons that haunt the day and darken the night with no light beyond the shadows. There are no shadows; there is only night. There are no stars, there is no moon, and there is only heavy air that sucks the life out of my soul.

Winter's darkness dulls my eyes.

Chapter 5

Spring

Drive and sing, stop and gaze, sit and watch. What am I watching for? I am watching the world pass me by. I have nowhere to go and nowhere to be. I threw away so many things in the heat of moments when the tears seemed to never stop flowing. After the mileposts passed in between the blur of tears, the screams of anger and the loudness of the blaring music, I suddenly had no idea where I was, much less where I was going. It seemed as if the mountains had disappeared in a blink of an eye, and the road opened before me. I knew this journey before me led nowhere, but there it was, calling me, challenging me to take its path that led far away from everywhere I had ever been. I pulled over and finally flipped off the music that had been blaring for miles and hours.

I climbed mountains until my leg shook and some tiny bit of fear set in. Would I make it home, would I make it back, and did it really even matter? I sat on boulders, rocks, and ledges, feet dangling, willing gravity to take me, willing the wind to lift me up and let me soar away where I could find peace without pain. I lay back on the hardness of the rock beneath me, eyes shut, feeling the sun burn my skin, yet never keeping me warm. All the while wondering why I felt so much pain and inside of me there was nothing but emptiness. I had given up; I was only being, and this was no way to live.

I don't know when or why I made a choice, but I did. I would go back and live a dream; I would take a chance. Maybe somewhere along the line things would change… I would feel, I would be, I would matter.

This is where it all began, and this is where it all shall end.

Chapter 6

Winter

Thirty years earlier....

It was dark in the room, and I wasn't comfortable. I wanted to turn on the lights, but I didn't know why I was afraid. I lay there quietly in the bunk wondering why I was even here. I wanted to go home, and I wanted to stay. In the stillness I realized that home was just a place and that the concept of "home," warmth, security, trust, and peace, was foreign to me. That's why I stayed where I was; that's why I came to be here. I was looking for a place not to call home but to be home. I was still looking.

There was a knock on the door. Parties at the NCO Club were winding down. I had just gotten back. The stares and the sexual innuendos where flattering, yet intimidating. I still had so much to learn. I wanted to be sexy, smart, and fun, yet I knew I was just trying to fit in. I wasn't any of those things. I was having fun on the dance floor. Then the touching started; the guys were getting too close. I had laughed and smiled until all of a sudden I couldn't breathe. I had gone back to the table, took a sip of my drink, and while no one was watching, I left. I had an overwhelming need to be behind a locked door. I will never know how I could have been so naive as to open that door.

I don't remember his name and I don't remember his face, but I do remember the thunderous echo of tears and the shame when I closed my eyes and willed myself to be anywhere but here. I remembered the pain after and the moment I knew when my soul was permanently charred and my body stiff and tenderm yet unmarked. I remembered sitting on the ledge outside the barracks room for days and days after. I remembered watching the sky from the ledge, watching the clouds roll into one, and wondering why they wouldn't envelop me in their nothingness. I don't know why I never said anything. I don't know why I was so afraid and ashamed. I just knew he was gone within the next few days, and I never saw him again. He was transferred out, finished his tour, and left the unit; I just knew he was gone. That was all that mattered then.

I never talked about that night, and I never thought about it; I never realized it was always there in the back of my mind, tucked away with speckles of memory that only haunted me in shadows of time. It was the stale smell of Cognac, the hands pushing and holding me down, the suffocating, and the inability to move or make a sound. It was the fear of being held down, and confined, and the fear of having anything over my face. Throughout the years that fear intensified, and now I know why I sometimes do the things I do.

That life wasn't home; this adventure was tarnished like old silver left behind in an abandoned castle. So I made time go by sitting on that ledge outside the barracks room where the nightmare began. Now I know why the mountains made me feel safer. The ledge was my first rock, my first mountain, and the first place I could dangle just beyond gravity's reach. There was room around me. There was enough of a visual field I would notice anyone or anything that came within my now vast personal space. Even though the way out was down, there was always a way out if the air became too crowded.

Maybe this was home. The ledge was home, where it was solid beneath me. The ledge with nothing but space around me, where the air was void of the bitter taste of tears and sweat and the stale smell of fear and shame. There was only me, and I was the only one who knew the way off that ledge was safer than the way on. I just had to take it. Instead, I stayed on the ledge every chance I got. Throughout life I found more ledges, more rocks, more mountains, and more places to sit and let time pass by and the bitter memories float off into the vastness of the clouds.

Winter's hollowness darkens in my eyes.

Chapter 7

Fall

Years later…

I was a shit magnet, which is a not so politically correct way of saying I usually got called out on my "on-call" schedule. It was the story of my life, luck of the draw, or a good thing because I still couldn't sleep anyway. The call came in around 3 A.M. I was awake; it was some kind of a nightmare where I felt I was being suffocated; it was the one that I had once or twice a week.

Sexual assault - this one was real; this one had just happened. The sexual assault calls were usually a child. It was some monster who the child called "father," "brother," or "uncle" who had molested him or her. The child would remember and start acting out. The monster, it seems, was always claiming innocence. The cases were always so hard to prove when the victims were anywhere from 3 to 17 years of age. The older they were, the longer ago it had happened.

This victim was in her home. She thought she was safe there, she was mature, and she was 74 living with her 95-year-old mother.

I drove up to find the amby (ambulance), the shift sergeant, and two deputies standing outside.

It was a small house, comfy looking. The furniture was old but clean, and everything was tidy, just a little outdated. The front door opened into a living room. There was a hallway to the right, a kitchen adjacent to the living area, and a small step to the left that led into a smaller hallway and into the victim's bedroom and bath. Off to the right of the house was where the older woman slept. I would find out later that she was fine and had slept through the attack. There was no sign of a struggle in the front living room. I was told the suspect had broken into the victim's bedroom window, spread his terror, and simply walked into the hallway and out the front door.

It was 4:30 A.M.

I walked into the victim's closed off bedroom. We had to preserve the evidence, so I was the first one in after she had left. One of the deputies told me that when the suspect walked out the front door, the victim had gotten up, saw the front door open, closed the door, checked to find her mother safe and still sleeping, and then went into the kitchen to call 911. I would figure it out later; she was one of the strongest women I would ever meet.

The window in the room just adjacent to the bed was broken. The bed was to the left of the window; blankets, comforter, and pillows were strewn beside the bed. There had been a breeze outside the house when I arrived, yet the curtains hanging inside the broken window were still. There was an eerie quiet, and I have to say, the hair on my arms and the back of my head stood up. I knew something terrible had happened in this room; I could sense the terror simply looking from the window to the bed. I would have known even if I hadn't been told.

There was one pillow leaning on the wall where there should've been a headboard. Camera in hand, I started photographing the bed. As I got closer, I saw the blood. It was on the pillow, it was on the sheet, and it was wiped on the wall. All I could think was that she was 74 years old; the bastard had to be caught. It wouldn't have mattered how old she was, actually, it was the point. She was 74, she was someone's grandmother, and for the first time, it was personal. Maybe it was the house, maybe it was the outdated décor, or maybe it was the smell when you first walked in where you knew someone older lived here. Someone who had lived life years before you or me; someone who had probably lived through so much good and bad, loved, and lost. Someone who had survived; someone who should have been respected for those few facts plus so many more. I didn't know her; I knew nothing about her. It was as if in one half second, time stood still, and I could see my grandma who was comfort and strength and home. It was a crime, it was a tragedy, and it was wrong; it was evil, and it was so disrespectful. She was 74.

Crime scene photographed, door shut, room closed off, feelings set aside -check. My presence was requested at the hospital. The victim just wanted to go home. Maybe she would talk to me-as a woman.

Chapter 8

I rushed to the hospital. As I walked into the ER, into the little space behind a curtain, she was there on the hospital bed. The first thing I noticed was the long and immaculately manicured fingernails on the tips of frail hands. Her top and bottom lips were the size of a golf ball on the left side. She was arguing with the ER doctor, telling him she was fine and needed to go home. She looked all of 100 pounds, and yet there she was telling my partner to "just get the bastard."

I told her who I was; I told her I had to ask her questions, and I told her to please listen to the doctor. Then, I don't know why or how or the exact moment, I just looked down, and I was holding her hand while the ER doctor put stitches inside and outside her lip; and she was holding mine.

This is what she told me. He had a knife. He put his hand over her mouth, and he told her he'd kill her. She didn't even hear him come in the room. She had "sensed" something and opened her eyes to see him standing at the foot of her bed. She struggled, he held her down, and she fought. He was too big, and she could still hear his voice. After he left, she waited a moment and then got up to check on her mother. She found the front door open and candy wrappers on the floor. He had just walked out the front door as if he had been invited, taking some of the candy with him.

He came in the door, he held her down, and he told her she wanted it. He was too big, he held me down, I fought, he was too big, and I could still hear his voice; I could still smell him. He just walked out the door like he belonged. Suffocating , humiliating, frightening…put it aside and move on because it was probably your fault anyway. It was a memory, it was a nightmare, it was real, and it happened to someone else. I was there, I saw the wounds, I saw the evidence, and it was now my responsibility to make it right. I had to make sure it mattered, and I had to make sure the wrong was acknowledged; I had to make it right.

I made a promise, "I will do everything I

can to catch this guy. I will do everything to make sure he pays. I will do everything I can to help you feel safe again." Ten years later, I wonder if I ever did. I wonder if she ever slept. I didn't.

Summer's colors have dulled to bleak browns in my eyes.

Chapter 9

Summer

One tiny piece of DNA, one tiny spot on a blue comforter that I knew had to be there took hours to find. One search warrant, one knife, one shirt, and one used up cigarette butt. One long conversation with the lab trying to get a rush on the DNA; just one match to the DNA on the comforter was all we needed. Just one match so she could sleep.

We had a guy. Everyone has a guy. But it was him, and I knew it. The first time I saw him, he acted confused and lost. When he turned his head to look at me, I wanted to smash it into the wall. The eyes are a mirror of the soul; his were glazed and empty.

So we traveled to his hometown. We spoke to his family and read his prior arrests. While talking with the local officers, we found out they only had a couple sexual assaults. One wasn't solved and one involved some man walking through the local department store scaring children with his verbal sexual innuendos.

I searched the local paper for information on the department store incidents. I checked the police report. It was our guy. I knew it and I could feel it.

When I interviewed him he was wearing a similar shirt that our victim had described. He even talked about the department store incidents. It only made me happy because I was right; it was him. But he said "I didn't rape no old lady." It was my job to prove he did. It was my job to make no mistakes. It was my job to make it right.

In a blur it was over. There was one DNA match on a comforter I had looked at for what seemed 100 times. There was one search warrant, one nine page arrest warrant, and one call to whoever was in the area to pick his sorry ass up. I didn't even want to wait for myself to get in the car and go. I just wanted him picked up. But I was the only one who knew what he looked like, so I had to wait for me anyway.

By the time I got to the residence where he was hiding, the other officers were ready to go. They entered the front door, which was opened by another guy, and they started to search the residence. I was standing outside watching the back door with another officer. One of the officers updated us on the radio; no sign of the suspect.

A few seconds later, it was as if the sky just opened up, the sun smiled, and the cotton clouds puffed up and became whiter than the mountain snow. It was spring. There he stood, our guy, on the balcony, ready to jump, and ready to run.

I couldn't help it, I said, "Well hello, going somewhere?" while the other officer said, "He's on the balcony; come through to the back." "Is it him?" me, "affirmative," and then the words we long to hear while walking the thin blue line, "you are under arrest," and the subtle, yet explosive, click of the handcuffs. We had our guy.

Chapter 10

Summer's Warmth

Years later…

I miss my mountains. I know they're not mine, but I had some certain spots. I miss the quiet peace of sitting on my rock, my ledge, and allowing my thoughts to run rapid. I miss stroking my dog behind his ears and the way he turned them towards me when I would start rambling about the beauty of the mountains. I miss his silent comfort. I miss the happiness in his eyes when he waited for me to catch up. We would sometimes sit, and I felt like I was on top of the world; it was so safe there, so quiet. It was the only place I could find peace. My dog would sit beside me and watch. I always wondered what he was watching for, and I always thought he saw what I did. Golden browns, vivid greens, and oh how the sky would be so blue and then so full of stars. I would find shapes in the clouds just before the sunset. He would nudge me with his wet nose, lay down, and then I would rub his shoulders while I picked out shapes and named them off. It was spring and summer all rolled into one. I was alone on those ledges, but I was never lonely. I felt secure and safe. The longer I walked, the higher we went, and the harder we climbed, the nightmares would just slip behind us. I could breathe. I didn't flash back to all the broken spirits, my own broken soul, and winter would go away, if only for a little while.

It was always summer in the mountains. Whether we treaded through snowy trails or climbed icy pathways, it was always summer in the mountains. When I was there, it was always summer in my soul.

In my eyes, summer's warmth is abundant.

Chapter 11

Fall

It happens when I least expect it and sometimes even when I do. One of my closest friends is dying. The doctors gave him two months maximum. He's called Hospice; his family is coming into town. I haven't known him for 30 years or ten years or all my life; I have known him for about four. I've seen him every week, sometimes once, sometimes twice. We spend ten minutes or maybe 30, talking shit or talking real life. We don't go out, we don't see each other, but for those few times since I met him, he has been my friend. He has listened; he has shown empathy, encouragement, and understanding. He has encouraged me and lectured me.

He knows what the smell of death is. He knows what it smells like after someone burns or someone bleeds to death. He has had nightmares, he has felt he accomplished a lot in life, he has no regrets, and he wants to die with his head up and his eyes open; all the while he is fully aware.

He is 84, he is a retired fireman, he is a Veteran, and he has been my friend. I love him. I am sad. I am proud that he tells me he loves me. I am grateful when he tells me I really am a good person and that I should always hold my head high. I am encouraged when he tells me that it will get better and that I must be positive and that I must remember that I am strong. He has been honest when he tells me that the nightmares may never end. He has told me when someone asks I should always say, "I'm great" even though I'm not. Eventually even I will believe it he says.

I will miss him for all these reasons and for the simple fact that he has been there. He was my ledge. I would look forward to him coming in to the place we liked to eat and socialize. I have cried silently on his shoulder, and he has cried silently on mine. It was not for what we have seen, but for what we have accomplished; even though our paths did not cross until our main journey was complete.

To my friend – I love you. I will miss you. I am sad but will try so very hard not to be.

You are not afraid, you do not have regrets, you have told me you love me, and I need to stay strong and keep moving on. To my friend, thank you for listening to me, thank you for loving me despite my faults, thank you for understanding my pain and for being empathetic to my nightmares. Thank you for encouraging me. Most of all, thank you for being my friend.

Fall's shadows hide the sadness in my eyes.

Chapter 12

Winter

Sometimes I can sense when someone dies. I've driven up to crashes and regardless of what the vehicles looked like, I could tell if the driver or passengers came out alive. I could tell if they died. I couldn't predict what happened after they left the scene, but I could tell you if someone had ever died there before.

It was late one night, a car had rolled over into a ravine, and the driver and one passenger said they were the only ones in the car. They were seated on the pickup tailgate of someone who passed by and stopped to help.

The vehicle was only about six feet down and laying on its side. Someone had to go down and make sure there was no one left in the vehicle or around it. Believe me, people lie.

It was about 2 A.M., the night was dark, and the mountain blocked the moon and stars. The slope at the start of the ravine was steep, the ground slippery from the weight of the vehicle as it careened down. All I cared about at the time was that I didn't fall on my ass in front of the other deputies. Of course I was selected and ordered to go down and check the vehicle and the area around it. The unspoken question from the boys was whether I could handle it. My unspoken answer was always yes, I am Army strong.

I slid down, managed to stay upright and was able to walk over to the vehicle. When I was approximately three feet away, I didn't want to move closer. You know the feeling, when the hair on the back of your neck stands up? What I felt was that and more.

The goose bumps on my arms were prominent in the night's breeze; the urge to flee was overwhelming, and every single hair on the back of my neck, or particle of, was standing on end as I shined the flashlight towards the vehicle. The night air cooled and what little light the moon had provided diminished. I knew death had been here. I knew even before I saw the one thing in front of me, the dirty and crushed teddy bear that lay partially under the vehicle. It's ribbon torn and dirt covered; its eyes solemn and sad.

I climbed up the ravine, my heart racing, trying to act calm when I felt like death's darkness was right on my heels. Later, I was told that two years prior, on the same night, in that same spot, death had been there. It had claimed the life of two young girls. Yet on this night, death had been out claiming another because the people that had been in the car on this night simply walked away. Why or how was it that I knew that even before I was told?

Everyone may not know that blood smells. It's almost metallic. A death that has occurred more than a few hours, depending on the weather, can smell anywhere from bad to downright nasty. But most people are surprised when they come across death. It's the shock of a still body, cold to the touch, and maybe a little blue or pale. This is also all dependent on the cause. What bothers me the most is knowing it's there before I see it; it's feeling death before it stands before me, and it's sensing death before it's visually there.

One time I drove three hours, 2,000 feet

up from 7,000 searching for a crashed plane. I felt it as I got closer, even though I had no idea how close I was. Death. It's quiet and serene; it's chilling and sudden. That is what death feels like. It's like nothing I've ever felt before. It's like nothing I ever want to feel again. But I did, and I do, and yet I go on.

Winter's coldness empties the heat from my eyes.

Chapter 13

Spring

The nightmares come though not on a regular basis. When they do, I wake up shaking, sweating, or chilled, and at times, frightened and screaming. In that first split second of awakening, I am still in the nightmare; I am still struggling to survive whatever terror has haunted my dreams. I search for the warmth of my dog's fur, the feel of his paw on my arm, the soothing sound of his nearly silent whimpering as he tries to save me from yet another confusing and frightening dream. His head lays on my chest, his eyes soft and so full of love and strength. He is so brave to come near me; he is so faithful to do so every time the demons come in the night. It's like being on the mountain with him. It's like sitting on the ledge watching over the earth while stroking the back of his ears. He is safety, he is strength, and his love is constant. I have yet to experience as pure a love. When I lost him, I lost part of me. I lost a piece of my soul, and I lost peace. There is no doubt in my mind that the bond between a human and a dog stretches further than the stars. I will never have a better friend, a better companion, or a better teacher. Without him, the nightmares come more often; they're colder and darker, brighter, and more vivid. Sometimes they come during the day, and I feel trapped, and I need to run because the pain that causes may force the visions away.

I remember less and feel more. All my senses are electrified, and I seem to hide even more. I can't explain myself, I can't feel myself, I don't know myself, and I feel so utterly and totally alone. I can't stand feeling invisible. I want to yell and scream, "Here I am; I am here," but the words won't come, and I feel myself sinking into the hole. So I run. I run to where the air is, and I run to where I can breathe. The only hard part is remembering what it was that made me run.

The promise of spring brightens my eyes.

Chapter 14

Winter

I saw a trash bag today and pieces of trash scattered around. People are so messed up. They litter, and they just leave it for someone to see and to smell. It's rotten and sickening. The black trash bag has blue ties. The bag is weighted down by liquid, and under the tree across the way, I see the head. Its eyes are looking at me, and its eyes are gazing towards the black plastic bag where the rest of the body is hidden. There are several bags now, and the smell is overwhelming, and the goo runs around my feet. It's spreading upwards, and the smell suffocates me, and the eyes are still staring. I run. I don't want to see it again, and I don't want to feel the coldness on my shoulders, and I definitely don't want to analyze it again. Yet it stays there, and I can't get that scene out of my head. I wonder why it didn't seem to bother me back then. Today it was only a broken doll that someone threw out in the trash. Its body was torn apart by some unknown little boy who was only tormenting his sister. Its plastic eyes were staring at me, unmoving, and its little painted smile was dirty from sand and bits of grime from leftover food packages.

A rancher saw a head under a tree . A woman's head with black bags with gooey liquid seeping out. When I got there I saw the bags, and for some reason, I couldn't smell anything. I guess my senses shut down except for my sight. I remember her head, swollen, bloodied, hair matted, and eyes open. It was so unreal and so clearly severed. Her head was under a nearby tree. The animals had rummaged through her bagged body parts, dragging off what they wanted and leaving behind what they couldn't take. There was not a lot there to analyze, and there was not a lot there except her head. Good thing they left her head behind so we could find out who she was. Maybe it was too heavy to drag further, or maybe they were interrupted, or maybe the liquid body parts were easier to get to.

We walked the area, searching for an

arm, or a leg, or a hand. We were looking for pieces of a body, looking for pieces of flesh while her soul hovered over us crying, begging, and in so much pain. All I could think about was who in the hell made black trash bags with blue ties, and I hoped like hell I would never see those kinds of bags again.

But it happened. I saw some under that tree left for the trash truck. I had that need to run, that need to find out what the hell happened here. I saw the lines of searchers sifting through the weeds looking for one more piece of flesh or one clue, and those black plastic bags started leaking rotted human flesh. Sometimes I can smell that scene. Think about leaving some chicken breast in the refrigerator and then forgetting to cook it in time, so you have to throw it out. Don't do that because then it has to be wrapped in several plastic bags, and a plastic baggie, because of the smell, even slight, brings back that day. The pictures in my head make me angry and sad and confused all at the same time. Then I'm slamming things and snapping at whoever is around and all the while screaming,

"I DON'T KNOW WHAT'S WRONG WITH ME!!" But I do. I just know that you really don't want to know; you really don't want to see what I see because the stupid chicken didn't get cooked in time. And I feel guilty and sad because I can't explain it and because I don't want you to know, and I don't want you to see a head under a tree and stinky liquid body parts seeping out of black plastic bags with blue ties smelling like the damn chicken I didn't cook in time. So it's my fault I'm frantic. You tell me to calm down. Please don't tell me to calm down when those pictures are swarming through my head, and the smells are overwhelming.

Winter brings its chill to my eyes.

Chapter 15

Summer

When you trust someone, when you allow someone into the tight circle of trust, it's like the long lasting brightness of summer. It's feeling like a child and running through the field freely. It's like the feel of your favorite blanket at grandma's house or the smell of chocolate chip cookies fresh from the oven. It is a feeling that is so far from the cold, bitterness of winter. There's trust, colorful balloons sailing in the clear blue sky. Then there's betrayal, lies, and secrets; it's when those beautiful bright balloons suddenly burst with the sound of gunfire or flash bombs and fall screaming into the night. You can duck, you can try to fight, and you can take cover, but all the debris just rains down upon you until you can't catch a breath. Your heart races and in your mind's eye, that comforting blanket that warmed you at grandma's is now tattered, torn, and faded. The little pink flowers that decorated the blanket in peace are now blood splattered. The blanket is now faded and worn, not necessarily from use but from years of journeys and seasons. I remember when I could pull that blanket from storage or off the shelf and wrap it around me when the pain rocked me or the bitter taste of tears froze in the coldness that I had become. Somewhere along my path, it stopped working. It's just an old worn out blanket. It's been patched and re-sewn so many times it has lost its warmth. It is like me, like the cold dark winter season that seems to have set in my soul. The journey goes on and on, and I take what I can. I remember trust, I remember peace, and I remember when it was spring and summer and there was nothing else but time:

When I am with you, time stands still
There is simply a moment
A moment that draws me tight into security, into peace
Within those moments there is no haunted past, no distant future
There is no you, there is no me, there is us

There is peace and joy and wonder
There is light and sparks and fire

There is truth, there is freedom to be, and there is love
It doesn't matter what the day was, what tomorrow brings
Or that yesterday is lost
It only matters that you are with me
That your hand feels secure, your arms comforting
The sound of your voice mesmerizing
The feel of your touch electric
The passion in your eyes consuming

I can't stop the passage of time
I can't stop time when it insists on moving on
I can't change what tomorrow brings or what yesterday brought you
Or that maybe part of today was lost
I can only promise that within those moments
There will forever be us, only you and I
There will never be distance or fear
There will always be faith and belief, love and peace
Within those moments I will give you all that I am
And when time moves on and those moments pass
I will continue to give you my trust, my faith
I will believe in you, I will comfort you, I will stand beside you

*I will support and guide you should you reach
for my hand
I will love you in those moments and far beyond
For today and for tomorrow
Not only for whom you are but also for what you
have brought me*

*Time isn't the enemy for it has given us moments
as these
If only for a moment, time has stood still so that
we can simply be
What I cherish most in this world, in this life, is
my time with you*

No worries, no nightmares, no loud confused voices, no bone chilling coldness. We can travel through the night watching the stars and chasing the moon. We can stop the car in the middle of the road and dance around the glow of the headlights. You don't tell me I'm stupid or it's silly, and you don't roll your eyes or grab my arm and pull me back into the car. You get out and laugh. You grab my hand as we swirl through the moonlight until you feel the shaking in my leg and you gently guide me back to the car where we sit quietly in the night. Our backs against the windshield, my head on your shoulder, and the sound of our breaths plays background to the music of the crickets still dancing in the darkness. We don't speak, we don't kiss, we simply are; we are simply being. You don't ask me if I'm okay; you know I'm not. You don't ask me why I dance too hard or run circles too fast; you accept I need to. You don't tell me not to cry; you just let me. Sometimes you cry, too. I don't tease you; I know your tears are real. I just take your hand, and the warmth radiates through us. Time stands still. There is only us.

My eyes sparkle with summer's warmth.

Chapter 16

Winter

And then winter returns with a vengeance.

After the calm comes the storm
Like the pain that follows the tears
And like the darkness that reflects the solitude
Sitting in silence....waiting
Waiting for love lost to somehow return
Along with peace, joy, and contentment

But the storm comes again and again
Bringing with it the pain...
Spinning in turmoil
Watching life's treasures lose their value
Becoming unidentifiable pieces of destruction
Twisted steel after the earth shatters
Dreams, hopes, passion swallowed up
By whatever lies beneath the ground
There I stand
Wrapped in my own arms
Watching the sky become a sinister orange
Knowing it's the eye of the storm

Teasing...conning
Waiting in fearful anticipation
Finally sure for one more time...
Sure that the worst is yet to come.

0700 and so far the morning has been quiet. There's even time for coffee and scones before going to check in with the DAs. I like the stillness after shift change. Night shift has gone home or is quietly finishing reports so that they can. Day shift is out patrolling for anything or nothing at all. Maybe they want to save whomever they can; maybe they just want to make it home another day.

I heard the "unattended" call. I heard the call for the coroner. I think it's just sad that someone died alone, found hours, days, or weeks later when it suddenly occurred to an old friend or co-worker to check on him or her because her or she hasn't been seen anywhere for some time.

First the welfare check; neighbors "notice" a car hasn't moved for days, or the postman asked if their neighbor is out of town and forgot to stop the mail. They notice the papers on the porch, the empty trashcan on the street, and the eerie silence when they knock on the door.

I know she's in the bathroom. I know I don't want to go through the door, but I'm Army strong. I see the quaint kitchen in the small cottage. I can tell a single person lives here. The countertop is clear of clutter, and there's one solitary pair of snow boots by the coat rack, one single cup by the sink, one computer open on the table, and a doorway at the opposite end of the room. There's a small but full-size bed neatly made inside that doorway. There is one well organized closet with only female clothing. I see just one nightstand with reading glasses and a dog-eared book that's probably been read several hundred times neatly stacked on the scratched up top. There's another door, it leads to what has to be the bathroom. It's open.

I can't smell anything but the cedar from the closet and a hint of spice smell from what was probably last night's dinner. It was a little chilly until I walked through the doorway into the bathroom, one little step across the threshold and into death's cold stillness.

I had been told that when a body hangs, the neck actually stretches. No one bothered to tell me that a human neck could suddenly look like a comic giraffe. Elongated, thin, and tight but still holding the head to the shoulders. Tongue loose and pale protruding from thick and bruised lips. I never knew a body's neck could get that long. I can only say it sucks to see it.

There she was, hanging with a belt from the shower, body sitting in the bathtub, fully dressed. She looked normal except for her damn neck, and she was in the tub with clothes on. Neat and tidy just like the front room. No note. No signs of erotic asphyxia. Another lonely person who made the choice that the end was here. Guts or stupidity? It didn't matter then. It was just a body. No person there; nobody home. It's kind of like how I would sometimes feel. No, nobody home here.

Then the radio announced another unattended.

Chapter 17

Winter

Upon arriving to the upper middle class home, somber deputies were standing at the front walk outside the open door handing out Vicks. One of them met us at the end of the driveway. "It's bad. Be prepared," was all he said. A couple more steps and then it was as if a switch went on. All my senses were assaulted with the chilling, rank smell of death, and the strong metallic smell of blood. I hadn't even made it to the front door.

I immediately was assigned to talk with the witness, the wife. The "boys" didn't think I could handle the scene. I'm stubborn and I'm hell-bent on doing my job without all the girlish remarks, so I walked in anyway.

Blood soaked bodies are inherently different in reality than on television or movies. In the movies or TV, the first thing you do is turn your head and say "that's nasty." When you're standing there, it's surreal. I thought for sure I'd throw up from the stench, but I didn't even have the urge. I just walked around the body on the bed, careful not to step in the coagulated pools of dark rusty black blood. How utterly bizarre that this person (well, once was) picked up that carving knife, was smart enough to hold it horizontal so as not to dull it by a hitting a rib, and continuously stab his own chest at least five times. The body really does hold a lot of liquid; it was seeping through the mattress into the carpet, permanently staining the floor underneath. Oh, and thoughtful enough to only wear undies. I'd say he's dead.

I still don't understand how he could stick himself so many times. Didn't it hurt? Was it an unconscious jerk response at the onset of that first stick? These are the questions I ask while I'm shooting film. It's apparent that unanswered questions are my unconscious response to things I can't grasp. I had plenty. Why do you think the knife landed there? Why do you think he took his pj's off? Don't you think it was kind of nice that he did it here and not in the master bedroom? I'd never have steak knives in my house after this. Would you? I didn't know the heart was that close to the skin. Did you? Do I have to go to the autopsy? Can't I just go start my report? So many unanswered questions. The only one that got answered was yes, the heart is that close to the ribs, which would make it close to the skin depending of the level of fat. I learned that in the autopsy. I also learned that peeling faces off skulls is something I don't want to see again.

Chapter 18

Winter

These are the visions I see in the night. A bodiless head, staring at me with dull eyes full of questions. A stain on the carpet which suddenly floods the entire ground with pulsating screams and boney fingers reaching up to me. Intact, yet broken puppets, their heads limp, arms and legs bent at odd angles sleeping in distorted twists of metal and steal. A woman with elegantly beautiful nails painted black dripping bits of flesh and blood screaming at me with wordless echoes.

Then there are the children huddled in an empty room, drowning in the guts of their tattered teddy bears. Their mouths gaping in silent screams while their private body parts are engulfed in flames. I'm running to the open door, but it's like running through a funny house. First I'm in the open emptiness, and then I'm slamming into a brick wall. My hands and feet are blistered and scratched. I'm dragging my lower body, pulling myself up, and crumbling down again with broken legs. The pain is unbearable, but I have to get there. I have to tell them all, "Be at peace. You are not to blame." Then it's me. I'm running, too, so I try to turn around to see if the nightmares are still there. My body jerks in circles. I'm fighting, I can't breathe, and all around me are endless walls cracked and weathered with age. I don't know where I am much less where I should be going. But I'm a warrior, and I keep getting up; why the hell do I never make it out of the empty well??

I don't know why I do the things I do. I don't know why I see the things no one else seems to, and I surely don't know why the need to fly or fight never goes away. The need to fly is winning, though. The solitude of the mountains is calling. There's cheering in my head, "run, run, run…."

Chapter 19

Winter

I am sitting at a concert. I'm dreaming how I want it to be a normal night of laughter, fun, and the gift of music. Why am I searching the sky for demons that may or may not erupt the night in flames of fire and ashes? Why am I scanning the crowd for invisible signs of torture and terror? Why am I anxious to question the man behind me, or the women beside him, when I see their stone like faces full of judgment and fear? Why do I look upon them ready to apologize for the girl on the other side of me whose laughter and dancing only makes me smile. She is alive, and she is full of life; yet their insecurities soak into my skin, and I find myself saying "I'm sorry." I'm sorry for loving life, I'm sorry for loving this moment, and I'm sorry for suddenly allowing myself to smile. Whether it be the talent behind the song, the soulful happiness behind the dancing child women, the steadfast human like robots swaying in their seats, or simply the joy I feel knowing the crowd is safe because I checked the exits and the people surrounding the aisles. I can't take the condescending looks, the eye rolling, the smirks, and the frowns. I can't take the man behind me that cusses me out because my clap is too loud or my whistle too sharp. So I stand up, and I boldly face him with nothing in my hand but honesty. I feel such a strong urge to explain that I paid to come here, too. I am condescend of those around me and I am trying to remain as stoic as the robot beside you. I just need to feel the joy or the peace or the excitement of the moment. I apologize for the noise and for the laughter, and the whole time the anger inside me grows until it's my finger in his face. It's my anger he hears, and it's simply my look that makes him scatter off into the crowd. I'm proud then. Fear me.

I am the one who sees through you; I am the one who has yet to judge you but can still see the hypocrisy in your eyes. I am the one who will haunt you later in the evening when your guilt and embarrassment keep you awake as you lie quietly in the night. You find comfort in your bed, and you are secure in your home. As I stand and watch the crowd disperse in the moonlight, I am the one that had your back. I am the one who you see on the news the next morning. I am the one that watched your neighbor mourn the loss of his or her parent, and I am the one that listened to your child's screams when that demon stole his or her innocence. I am the one who picked the pieces of your best friend's body up off the pavement, and I'm the one who tried so desperately to pull your spouse out of the twisted metal because he or she was a tad bit late and took his or her eyes off the road for just one second to text you because you didn't answer the phone.

I'm the one who thought I could save the world. I am the one whose haunted dreams were once reality. I am the one who in a split second could set the record straight by making every one of my nightmares your reality. But I don't. I won't. Because someday, somewhere and somehow, your eyes will close indefinitely; be it before mine or long after. On your way to your final destination, you will have a glimpse of my reality; and for one brief moment, you will wonder how you ever felt powerful enough to judge what you knew nothing about. My screams are silent, and my anger boils barely beneath the surface of my skin. Don't look at me, don't glance my way, do not question my solitude; you have no idea what lies just below the exterior of my surface. Only I know when the fire begins to consume me, and only I know when there are no more cracks in the wall to climb upon. I am erupting. Please let me be; let me cool in the way only I know how. Let me fall, climb, and soar. Please just let me be. I am who I am. I can no longer change. I no longer have the need to. Let me be.

Yes, I hear voices in the night. Yet, they're not speaking to me. They are just loud and jumbled. It's as if there are six televisions on six different channels, and every single one is turned up to full volume. One of my doctors says it's the thoughts in my head. My head is full of turmoil, and when I lie quietly in the night, those thoughts start screaming because there is nowhere for them to go. I internalize and I'm overflowing.

Chapter 20

Summer

My child is three months old. I can't wait to get home and hold her. She is beautiful, and her chubby little arms reach for me when I walk in the door. Her arms are full of innocence, her eyes full of sparkle, and the gurgling speech that comes from her mouth pours warmth through my soul. It's summer.

I want to hold her tightly and feel her little heart next to mine. My favorite time is to lay her on my chest and rub her back as our hearts seem to beat together. To her I hum the songs in my head because I can't remember the words. Her butterfly lashes flutter and close, and there isn't a more peaceful place than this- my baby in my arms.

She will never know how I spent my day. I will never want her to. All I want in this world is for summer to stay forever in hers.

Earlier I had walked through the wintery tunnel of the base morgue, every step amplified, hushed voices sad and lost souls searching for whatever light that shines at the end of their journeys.

The box was small. I remember how it bumped from side to side in the van on the way to the airport. The tiny little box, secure in the back of the cargo van, seems to implode with the noise of an M16 at every corner or turn the van took. We couldn't speak because each of us were desperately trying to rid our memory of the sight of that little blue hand clutching the stiff cotton blanket inside the tiny little box.

Someone lost their today - on the eve of my daughter's third month birthday. Why I remember that day so vividly is beyond me. Why do I remember the sound of the box in the back of the van, or why do I remember the little blue hand that I had to see due to protocol when transferring a body? Why at times does it seem like years ago, days ago, seconds ago…Why do I hide behind that vision, and why does the memory sit beneath the surface of the wall I built….I don't know why; I just know that it does.

And later, as I lay quietly in the night,

I'm secure and safe in a warm bed. My child lay sleeping peacefully in the next room. I know in reality I am expected to feel safe, to rest quietly, and to sleep soundly. But I can't pull my eyes away from the partially open door. I hold my breath so as not to miss any one of the nights sounds. It's silent except for the hush of my quick inhale that I try to muffle with my cupped hand. Suddenly I hear a door open, steps on the thick carpet are magnified in the night's quiet. My eyes have adjusted to the darkness, and I see the silhouette of petite figure shuffling towards the open door of my baby's room. Suddenly I'm out of bed, flinging myself through the door frantic with worry and fear that my subconscious mind tells me it's ridiculous to feel.

"What are you doing? Where are you going? She dreams out loud at times. She's fine. I've got her. Don't touch her. You'll scare her." I know I'm being silly, and I know I shouldn't fear the silhouette in the night; yet my heart pounds, and my hands sweat, and I can't help but run to my daughter's side before my mother can pick her up. Why am I so protective? Why am I so afraid that the one person who gave me life will hurt the one I did?

It is because she didn't want me to bring her here; yet I know she loves her. What has happened to me that I can't let myself trust anyone at all? I cry silently while I rock my precious child in my arms. I promise her no one will hurt her, and no one will ever take her away. She is safe, and she is safe with only me. My mind whispers that I'm overreacting, but my heart screams that I need to. I'm confused and sad and hurt, and I realize that my broken soul is still frozen in the depths of some distant winter storm. Is this why trust is far from my reach? Is part of me to forever be stuck in the snow bank that looms consistently over my reach?

Chapter 21

Winter

I am falling. I wake up screaming with the terror forcing my fingers to grip the blanket edge so tightly that my forearms ache. The tightening in my arms clears my head, and I realize I am safe in my own bed. I knew the doors were locked. I checked them several times before lying down. Sleep was so hard to come by; the nightmares seem to lurk in the shadows ready to pounce within minutes of closing my eyes. I rarely remember the night terrors that burst out of my skin the minute my screams wake me. I shake and I tremble, my breath quick and unsteady as my eyes regain focus and that ache in my arms awakens me.

Sometimes I remember I am walking through a house. It's empty and silent. I reach for the one closed door, and when it swings open, I scream. I don't remember what was inside, I don't remember if there was even anything beyond the doorway, and I don't recall being forced to open the door. Is what's inside so frightening that I really don't remember? Is it so real that my subconscious refuses to acknowledge it, or is it just another tragic memory that lies buried within my mind?

I breathe deeply. I don't reach for the light switch because I don't want to see what could be there without the darkness. I just breathe. I unclench my fingers. I will the daylight to come. Sleep is forgotten; tomorrow is another day. I will spend the first few moments of day trying desperately to remember what it was I saw behind that dream door. I will search my mind for where it was I walked within that dream. Every morning it haunts me until it slips from my memory like so many other things only to wake me again, screaming in the night.

Chapter 22

Fall

How does living my life weigh upon the conscious of someone else? How do my mistakes or my misfortunes make me inconsiderate of someone else? How is it that I am constantly longing for someone to believe in me, to feel secure enough knowing that someone has my back and that someone is at my side and has faith in me regardless of the outcome? I am alone. I am not enough. I never have been.

It isn't enough that I am kind. It isn't enough that I won't gossip. It isn't enough that I do the best I can to treat others the way I would want to be treated. It isn't enough that when I feel the ravages of war swoop down upon me that I breathe first and strike later. It isn't enough that I ignore that rage in my soul and walk away from battles. It isn't enough that once I turn the other cheek and get struck again, I come up swinging. It isn't enough that I hold myself steady and that I keep the evil at bay; when I scream in the night, I wake up fighting but can still that fight with what little breath I have left within me.

I can walk alone in the moonlight. I can listen quietly to the birds as they soar through the trees, and I can climb a mountain in pain and never give up; but I still can't ever seem to be enough. I'm not enough to hang onto; I'm not enough to fight for, to live for, or even to die for. I'm not enough to look at myself in my own mirror and smile at what I see.

I see pain. I see sadness. I see a broken soul and empty eyes. Yet, through all of that emptiness, I still see strength. I see a warrior, and I know deep within the steady beating of my heart that I will go on. I will always just keep going on. I will keep on moving; I will keep on walking, and I will keep on running. I will run to what I search for, I will run from what I lost, and I will never stop. There is no joy, no sorrow, and no fear. You wonder why I never sit still. I'm never enough, so I can never stop.

Chapter 23

She is screaming. The bed of the pickup tilts as the jaws of life try to break her free. I hold her hand, and I repeat over and over again, "Look at me, look at me, breathe with me. I won't let go."

Her eyes look into mine, and I know she sees her fear and pain mirrored. But I breathe and I am calm. Her screams quiet in the night's stillness. Flashlights flicker over the twisted metal of what was once a solid vehicle. The flashing lights from the emergency cars play eerily on the faces of the rescue crew. Their focus is uncanny. Everyone has a job to do. Mine is to make sure her screams quiet and her focus is on me.

She can't focus on the pickup that crushes her legs and holds her pinned to the ground. She can't focus on the blood that seeps down upon her. She can't focus on the carnage surrounding the crash or the glass shards in her hair. She can't focus on where she was supposed to be or what brought her here.

So I talk softly despite the noise of the twisted steel settling around us. I block out the metallic smell of blood, the saltiness of sweat, and the taste of my own fear. "Focus on me, look at me, breathe with me. I'm not letting go." I don't know if she hears me. I feel the weight of her hand in mine, and I see her eyes focus and her screams turn to whimpers until it is only the two of us trapped underneath what seems to be the weight of the world.

I have to focus on stilling my thoughts so she can't read the terror in my eyes. I wonder briefly if her legs are still there or if the pain she feels in them is only what once was. Will she walk again, will she survive, and will she scream at night like I do? "Look at me and breathe with me. I'm not letting go."

I never knew her name. I will never forget her face when I pass a crash on the highway and when I see the wooden crosses on the side of a different road. I see her face. I see her eyes. So I tell myself, over and over again, "Focus on me and breathe with me. I'm not letting go."

Chapter 24

Summer

The stars have drawn your smile in the sky. Through them I see the sparkle of your eyes. And I remember…

Here's to our souls that collided. Here's to the silent bond that held us together. Here's to the memory, here's to our memories, here's to our secret, and here's to what was once just you and me.

Here's to an empty bottle of Corona, one M&M of each color, and a single rose. I remember the stolen kisses, the electric feel of your hand in mine, and the way my heart melted when you looked at me. I remember talking until the sun came up, driving in the drop top, and racing through the rain. I remember the battles on the court, in the field, down the lane, and over the bonfire. I remember you, I remember me, and I remember the first time we discovered that the eyes are truly a mirror of the soul.

How I hated you. I hated that you looked my way but never said a word. I hated that you smiled at something I said but never acknowledged I said anything at all. I hated the depth in your eyes, the smile on your face, and the emptiness I felt when you looked away. I hated you.

How is it that I still miss you? How is it that at times I can still see your face, hear your laughter, and sense the darkness that creeps into your soul when the fall season ends? We were never meant to be, yet we were. We were rarely together, yet we were always one. Then you were gone.

There were no skid marks and no sign of a hurt animal, another vehicle, or a medical issue. Did you reach over to turn that one song up? Did you know that fall was over and decided it was time that you were, too? Did you feel pain, sorrow, joy, or nothing at all? I see it all in my mind's eye. I feel it all in the winter of my soul. It was another moment, just like those we always stole. There was one moment to feel everything and then nothing at all.

I see your broken and mangled body lying in the dirt and gravel. I see your car twisted into ravaged bits of steel and glass. I went to that tree, and I picked the last piece of perfectly rounded lug nut still buried in the tree where the bark had simply disappeared. It was kind of like you. I sensed you then, like that naked tree baring it's soul you stood there shadowed in the baking sun with your arms wide and your eyes dark and full of mischief and passion. As the wind whispered through the leaves, I heard your voice, "Keep your shades on even when you watch the stars. Catch the brightest one, and you'll find your big hug. I remembered you."

Years later, I found a place where I had everything I wanted. I search the sky at night and early mornings for the only constellation I know. I see it in the stars, some bright, some faded, but it is all there; the constellation of your smile, your eyes, your touch. And in that moment it is summer in my soul, and I am at peace.

I loved you, I hated you, I wanted you, and I needed you...

Today you are my friend

We sit by the fire in silence
Because you know I need space
But can't bear to be alone

We drive recklessly in the moonlight
And stop in the center of the road
Because you know I have to count the stars

Today you are my brother
You let me cry and you listen
Your arms are strong when you pull me up
The teasing sparkle in your eyes make me smile

We share laughter at something
Only we understand

Today you are my enemy
Your eyes cut through me
And make me shiver in the darkness
The coldness in your voice makes my anger grow

I want to see the pain in your eyes
When I throw the distance back at you

Today you are my lover
Your arms hold me tight
Your caress makes me quiver
I watch as your eyes grow warmer

I draw you closer
To savor the warmth, the safeness, the love

All in a day
You are these things to me
The friend I can laugh with
The brother I can lean on
The enemy I can battle with
The lover I can bear my soul to

All In a Day…

Chapter 25

There is nothing more than a moment. There are those that you take or those you have been given. I realize that now as I sit in my dream I created so many years ago. The stars glitter around me, the sun shines down on me, and the seasons surround me and draw me in. The winter coldness sweeps in at times as does the burnt brownness of fall, but the warmth of summer and the promise of spring tease me with the momentary warmth they create.

I still don't know where I am or where I belong. Yet in some of those moments when my senses are heightened, I know. I know I belong here with the land that grows hazy in the mornings chill and where the land speaks it's volumes begging me to watch it grow and change and then change and grow again.

At times the road calls to me. Take me and follow me to nowhere it calls. Take another journey and ride until you can ride no more. But I stay, secure in the solitude this land around me has created.

I tell you at times I am lonely. You said I asked for this life. You said I asked to be alone and that I asked to be alone with my nightmares, my thoughts, my fears, my failures, and even my successes. Just because I created my fortress doesn't mean I always want to be alone.

I still long for that someone to love me freely and to accept me for what I am. I long for someone to accept the coldness, the darkness, and at times, the light and the laughter that flow freely from within me. But I know it will never be, for you have reminded me time and time again that I am nothing but a bundled bunch of endings all rolled into one.

I have made my ending now. When I lie in bed at night I can feel my pulse beating through my veins. I try hard to cover my neck and my wrists. I know what would happen should someone sneak into my secure world and cut me there. The blood would pour out of my body and the emptiness would pour out of my soul. I wonder why I have to hide those parts of me. Am I really afraid of what may come to take me, or am I simply afraid of what I want to take

But I wrap my arms within the blankets tightly, and I secure my neck underneath the covers. I toss and turn and wonder what I am waiting for and why I can't find the peacefulness of dreamless sleep.

I'm still out there, somewhere, searching, wondering, feeling too much, and then again feeling nothing at all. I'm cold and shivering, yet hot and sweaty all at the same time. I reach over for the comfort of my dog's fur. His nose softly nuzzles me, and I know in that moment I am needed. I unravel the covers and brace myself to face another terror-filled night alone.

Chapter 26

I'm free. I'm falling. I'm not afraid. You may ask how my story ends. Is there more? Is there more terror, more cases, more hate, more love, and more seasons?

I can tell you now that there is nothing else. I have more nightmares. I have more than the plane crashes, the vehicle crashes, the rapes, the murders, the bombs, the assaults, and all the wickedness surrounding my existence, be it past or present or even future.

I know I will face more and overcome more. I will live a little more and die a little more inside. I know I will be alone, for I won't let anyone in as it isn't safe anymore. I'm not safe anymore.

As I lie awake at night, in the early dawn or the late evening, I will still grasp that tattered blanket from underneath a memory, and I will hold it close around my head. I will wrap it tightly around my arms. I will wonder as you may…is today the day I will take what destiny has brought me? Is today the day I will be no more? Or will I continue to simply be, knowing that there is nothing else but a moment and that truth does lie in that moment. And yes, knowing that the eyes are truly a mirror of the soul. Knowing that accepting what I am, what I have become, and what I will forever be is forever floating through the seasons of my soul. Winters, springs, summers, and falls. These are the seasons of the soul. They are the coldness, the hope, the warmth, the chills, and the consistency of changes in between.

I am constantly changing, I am constantly moving. The pain goes on and on. The fear of closeness, the anticipation of going beyond my secure space and my circle of trust also goes on and on. I can't sit still, and I can't sit down; the pain takes my breath away, so it's better to avoid even trying to be still. I move. I move around, back and forth, up and down, and around and around. I am running, and the circles are closing in on me. They are smaller and smaller until I won't have a circle; I will only have a space.

Within that tiny bit of space will be my

season. It will change at its own pace. It will warm me and chill me and promise me and take from me. My soul will hover, and then it will crash down upon me soaking its way back into my being. I will be that season in that moment of truth. I will be alone. I will survive, for every season of me has its armor. I am a warrior, past and present. I will overcome time and time again.

I can't predict the season you may find me in, and I can't promise it will be a season you should not intrude upon or one you will fear. I can promise that this is me. Truth is constant when my soul seasons speak. Whether terror filled or peaceful, whether cold and dark or warm and bright, these are the seasons of the soul.

Chapter 27

Post-Traumatic Stress Disorder sufferers are in a constant state of fight or flight. The main complaints are nightmares, emotional numbness, intense guilt or worry, angry outbursts, feeling on edge, and avoiding thoughts and situations that are reminders of the traumatic event. Brain analysis can show dysregulation in the frontal lobes, amongst other areas. The frontal lobes are involved in executive functioning, abstract thinking, expressive language, mood control, and social skills. That's what my diagnostic report says.

Seventy percent of adults in the U.S. have experienced some type of traumatic event at least once in their lives. Imagine experiencing more than one, for instance, three or four or even six. At last count, of the traumas I dream about, the ones that can even haunt my days, the ones that flash through my mind in any given season, there are 14. Those are the ones I have mentioned, talked briefly about, tried to describe, and longed to forget. I can live in the past when these memories haunt me. I see everyone or everything as I saw that one person or one thing that was unfathomable at that moment.

I am working toward overcoming the boundaries that the traumas I have witnessed have bestowed upon me. These are the seasons of spring and summer. I'm warm, focused, and living life. Then, like a bomb that bursts in an unexpected moment, winter or fall set in. I am again only focused on running. I run through fields of emptiness, streams of blood, and clouds of haunted memories. You may not recognize me, for these are seasons even I don't know why I do the things I do.

But those seasons pass, as do the warmer ones, and I go on; I go on and on. I am not weak. I am a warrior, always going on and on.

There are approximately 44.7 million people who were or who are struggling with PTSD. May they, too, never stop going through the seasons. May they never stop going on.